S A

METAMORPHOSIS

S A F E

METAMORPHOSIS

OTIS MENSAH

IN CELEBRATION OF LETTING THE PEN BLEED AND THE ART OF VULNERABLE EXPRESSION AS A VEHICLE TO A MORE SOULFUL HUMAN CONNECTION. WITH WHOLEHEARTED LOYALTY TO THE ALCHEMY OF RAP AND THE CULTURE OF HIP-HOP IT INHABITS; A CULTURE THAT TAUGHT ME TO HARNESS EMOTION WITH TOTAL CONVICTION AND TO MANIPULATE LANGUAGE FOR THERAPY.

FOREWORD

Beyond our mutual respect for Hip-Hop and hummus, myself and Otis both believe in a better world. A world with greater equality and tolerance where there is a niche for every one of us to help make that a reality. With that belief, and both of us living in a northern post-industrial city called Sheffield, we were bound to come together.

Strangers matter in Sheffield, because sooner or later it becomes clear that there aren't really any. We all know someone who knows someone who knows the person we now think of as a stranger. It is this idea, at its most simple, which helped me discover a burnishing passion to fight injustice. I got involved in politics because I was, firstly, tired of complaining and also frustrated by asking the wrong people to do the right thing. This led me to become a councillor, then Lord Mayor of Sheffield, and recently an MEP representing Yorkshire & the Humber at the European Parliament.

One of the things I am immensely proud to have done during my time as Lord Mayor was creating the post of Sheffield's Poet Laureate. Nobody suggested I should do it or gave me permission to do it. I just thought it was a great idea and wanted someone to champion Sheffield's creative arts in new and exciting ways, but to also really make a statement. For me, Otis represents all that is great about Sheffield and being a voice for a generation; he's vulnerable yet dynamic, skilful and radical. It's worth pointing out that while the response to his appointment was overwhelmingly positive, some comments made it clear that poetry is still massively affected by elitism; and has a long history of white male mediocrity. Yes, Otis is the first Hip-Hop artist to be awarded a poet laureate title in the UK, and I'm proud that he's breaking down barriers, smashing the stuffy stereotype, and reminding people that poetry is meant to be for the people.

At the heart of this collection of poems, Otis shows us that in a precarious, ever-changing world, the most radical thing we can do is be ourselves. He also shows us the power of authenticity and doing things differently.

Doing things differently can be scary, and there are people who will hate you for it, but there are also people who will love you for it and who will join you. You might even change the world, in small ways, large ways and middle ways in between, or spark others to do so – like Otis has and continues to do in inspiring me and so many others. But if you keep doing things how they've always been done, and if you stick to outdated traditions (and what is tradition if it isn't peer pressure from dead people?!) then you risk never knowing what it's like to succeed and to fail in the pursuit of great endeavours. So go ahead and enjoy this amazing collection of poems and I dare you not to leave feeling inspired. And let us make a promise, not to denigrate but to inspire. Rather than bemoan the present, let's paint a picture of what can be. Instead of inciting hatred and instilling fear, let's rise above the chorus of our age and dare to sing a different song.

– Magid Magid, former Lord Mayor of Sheffield

prototype publishing
71 oriel road
london e9 5sg
uk

Published by Prototype in 2020
Copyright © Otis Mensah 2020

The right of Otis Mensah to be identified
as author of this work has been asserted in
accordance with Section 77 of the UK
Copyright, Designs and Patents Act 1988.

Design by Theo Inglis
Illustrations by George William Stewart
and Miroslav Kiss

Typeset in Neue Haas Unica
Printed in the UK by TJ International

A CIP record for this book is available
from the British Library

ISBN: 978-1-913513-02-3

( )   (   )
 p   prototype

(type 1 // poetry)

www.prototypepublishing.co.uk
@prototypepubs

CONTENTS

LIKE THERAPY

It's like therapy to me
riding waves of systematic heresy at sea
rid you of that uninvited stranger that never leaves
empty houses and holes in stories lit up like
Tel Aviv at night

Life in the 21st century
where they pump my people full of corn syrup and fluoxetine
causing toxic dreams but
these words are like kerosene
that light up lanterns by my feet
so I can see and avoid this pier of brown broken glass
a town bestowed to clowns
in cloaks and masks
where rats and roaches laugh
at people coaxed by stats

A DAY CLOSER TO FOREVER

This world feeds us so much nothing
only to tell us you are what you eat

I envision echoes from impartial spectators saying
'Why so brash
rash
and hasty?'

I hear the voice of my mother calling
'Things aren't always as they seem,'
begging me to look beyond the shell we're all caged in
to me this is more than apparent

I recall all too well asking for black pudding
in hope of chocolate cake
as sniggers from a waiter render my childlike desires meaningless.
Now, if I could reincarnate into the me of past
I'd say,
'You, Sir,
are a dream killer,
a dream killer.'
I'd harden my shell
to protect me from the knocks of what is
to be whilst you
piss your dreams down the water well of life

Gazing at my reflection in a cracked piece of glass
it saddens me deeply that I'll never know what it is
to see myself as I truly am
I can only look upon a snapshot of myself
a billionth of a second into the past
They say 'time implies change and
change necessitates imperfection'
so I imagine a time where my todays,
yesterdays and tomorrows are all combined,

no one could tell me what I can't do
because of what I've done
or what I must do
because of where I've come
I said 'I imagine a time' but there would be no time
just existence
a line
journeying what it means to Be
silence but not deadness

a kind of calm out of reach for now
bound by space and time
where tweeters tweet
bloggers blog
and demons whisper
but every day when I wake
I look around at the walls which enclose me
and I say
today is a good day
a day closer to forever

Boy: I have a confession to make.

Moon: Tell me, child!

Boy: I've been trading in sleep for poems.

[INSERT SLEEP HERE]

I know you're tired
I've drunk the dry sip that never meets satisfaction
during glimpses I've felt decades of drought
I know all about the boulders that rest in wrinkles
forcing crooked smiles
I know the mass of moons in orbit rest on your weary back
I know how weight feels
I know the cliché that pressure makes for precious stones
but sometimes
sometimes we just break
we break before we meet esteem
still-births still happen to those born and grown

I'm standing on the back of an insect
and in all my power
I found all my insignificance
how life can just be stamped out

I remember the feeling
like cities raining down on my body
drops of water concentrated with people
buildings
iron curtains
time
metal debris
all this world's ills and its machinery
toppling down on my bare back

I know drowning makes it hard to stay awake
I thought about how to think
when your head's trapped in a tank of running water
but your body roams free
I remember gulping and gasping for help
but no one could break me out of myself
I was an insect too

I know how to forget to sleep
and when I keep my eyes open long enough
I see technicolour that isn't there

I stood on the neck of an arachnid
I felt what it feels to have no bones
no structure
just the space in between everything before and after

I know you're tired
I remember the feeling of helpless daze
I remember that sacrifice isn't always compromise

ODE TO BLACK THOUGHT

I had a dream that I went to see The Roots. The atmosphere was electric. Questlove played an eternal break of undoubted flavour to call out Black Thought, who rushed the stage like a floating spirit, both hurrying and taking time in one. Tariq was draped down in a black silk cloak that covered the whole stage. The cape of sorts was embroidered with red lines that ran parallel throughout the cloth like the blood vessels of midnight streets in Philadelphia and his cadence embodied revolution.

Like the dreams of my youth, where in sleep I sought out the validation of favoured artists, I woke myself with a croaked inner voice proclaiming, 'I NEED THAT'. I was speaking of the cape. If only I could wear its skin like my own and feel what it feels to be the sound of reverence and just rest, rest in it.

PONDERING
For as long as my memory can stretch, I've longed for what I now call my vision. Vision sounds somewhat social and less self-indulgent than the truth. What I truly speak of is a lonely dream. To tour the world, playing to crowded rooms of those who endorse spending nights in states of poetic escapism. To tour 300 days out of 360 and 306 a leap year. This leaves me with just 60 days to create and have to face the sore reality of sun reflecting on red brick when light can't cast away clouds fast enough.

FAMILY & FRIENDS
Just 60 days to meet and greet because Otis is such a busy artist, and back when the duty of school attendance burdened me, it was this dream that kept me afloat. I felt so uneasy. So denatured like a nuclear bomb in a lunch box. So asocial. So unsure. The dream whispered, 'Why conform? Peer pressure is for children without destiny.'
A purpose I possessed, but a purpose nevertheless, possessed me to isolation. My security net, my soul-nourishing medicine bottle for rejection, my Plan B to happiness, a way to be alone and never lonely.

I CONTEMPLATE THE DREAM

I have to confront myself with honesty, that my dream was fuelled by a fear of life; a fear to let myself live, lust, to be tempted, to meet with my anxiety. It's easy to deny yourself potential rejection and hurt.

AMBITION / DELUSION / ESCAPE

Something bigger. Something greater. Something around the corner. I am chosen. I am gifted beyond reason.

Through my bedroom window the city moves, it moves at night like sleep is reserved for small towns. It carries its self-importance in unwavering motion and when I wake the city never stands corrected, it moves unrested, moving to forget, moving to forget. This quality of moving to forget, I've built myself a life around like the city I inhabit. I'm so tired of forgetting and remembering not to be still.

The people that are attached to the branches orbiting my life are falling, left, right and centre. With every branch that falls, I'm reminded of my own stem and leaves. This tree I've grown tall with is temporal, unstable. I'm left facing the wind, shaking amidst the elements, knowing my branch could be next; my family and friends that I've ignored to chase dreams.

Stuck stubbornly to the chest of drawers by my bedside city-portal are two images. One of an MPC-3000 and the other a signpost displaying 'TOTALLY LOST'. These images conclude the narrative, at least for now. A battle for true intentions that feed my life with love and inspiration and a getaway plan; a runaway train, trailing uncharted territory.

SHADOWS AND VOID

Sat in sad times for social norms
I open up to get shut down
the computer crash
mother asking 'What mood is that?'
So I grip the pen to scribe these black thoughts;
The Roots is back

Rabbit holes and trapdoors
inside my cerebrum
where the cat claws scratch doors
search for gateways in emotional patchwork
every word on a chess board
not everything is black and white
where taboo is cliché
never seen it coming like Connect Four
can't detect wars on web stores
more harmony and less force
yes, please

No more tension headaches
binge-eating disorders
seeking for cause
cut me leave me in sawdust
write my name in these shavings
thesaurus tyrannosaurus
felt like the first to suffer
but a line of lovers before us
I hold this hole like it's home
I won't sell my soul for a tour bus
lend an ear to self
love and loath this land of the lawless
try and transcend to the centre
ascend to myself the former
end up where I started
future in drafts that are drawn and quartered

Tempted by touch;
some cacti that want to be hugged
but left me cut for this love like YO
you got me stuuuuuuck
now I'm sparring Jujutsu with Yoshimitsu
singing lullabies
a misuse of 'I miss you's
am I just another internet Confucius confused
no empathy for his shoes
got issues like a band or publications
h o l e s in communication
sink relationships
when virtue lies on the stretcher
where the patient is
all my people struggle for this
a lifetime searching for loopholes
there's no cheat-codes
my brother put me on perspective in a higher plane
he told me just to 'keep soul
and breathe slow'
so I hop on stage for therapy
but it turned into a freak show
I had a dream God said to me
'They make men out of things like you'
then I woke up with pockets of potential and
space in these shoes to fill
but I just keep filling them up with shovels of sand
castles crumble
dancing in puddles
so I sink where I stand

and we just keep normalising abnormality
in the name of social norms
as if majority and popular opinion equated to truth
but I won't keep feeding an emptiness that's never full
bite me

Pain gave birth to Art
although they never did see eye to eye
Art cared only for liberation from its predecessor

ALTERNATIVE SPACE

Travelling through alternative space
The Earnest is lurking in shade
in murky waters where the waves crash and dirty my brain
long jump black holes big enough to take up eternity's place
absurdity's grey
only certainty in black and white
I wear this Cage like a second name

A clerk by day
writer by night
trying to instigate insight
but there's nerves in my state
how to be fluid like water
sustain and
further my flame

HOPE

I saw the morning give birth to the day
from the moment our bodies were cursed
dancing on legs that are withered away
now we crawl in the dirt
just a pawn in the race
I've got nothing to say.

The change in time and space when shackles are made tambourines
when the song emancipates
the tongue that knows its cage and plays against its prison
spluttering beauty muttering freedom
sometimes whispers are louder
the meek that ripped roofs from houses
whilst your favourite rapper shouts at walls rubbing penis in hand
my feet in sand trying to understand roots
staring at our heroes like 'Oh you oppressor you'
'Oh you oppressor you'
unlearning and learning not to become one too.

The universe is introvert
the world is backwards
murder cattle
disperse the classes
weeping Saturn
falls from skies
life or death
we chose the latter

take our data
grow our status
failing fate
you know what happened
hate for hate
cycles, patterns
pay my way

find me tattered
play the game
count your castles
laden now
path is narrow
oozing sore
lost the battle

a new remorse
I'm off the saddle.

There's no backing down when the shofar sounds
sadly none but chauvinists around
and I don't get paid like Sofar Sounds
slinging rap jargon
I was given a bad bargain
speaking to sun in the back garden
and wrote what She told me
but my barter could only buy me fire emojis
and not more time like I'd hoped for
there's no more time like I'd hoped for
there's no more time like I'd hoped
there's no more hope.

SPEAK LIGHT INTO THE DARK

I'm not a rapper

I'm a catalytic converter

transforming external-world toxins into poems of hope

I caught my lows by the neck and saw them tangled in rope
at the gallows that never existed, just a thought when I wrote
The Valleys of Death tower high so I take one for the road
consume this text as we roll, they say it's food for the soul.

LISTEN, AND NONE SHALL DISFIGURE THE MESSENGER IN THE SENTENCE

I'm sleeping on tracing paper, sketching scenes from my dreams
sentence inside a bottle
it travels down streams of anguish
turns negligence into novels
and passes over resentment
resides in my mind colossal
expanding with every word
as thick as thieves with fallen thinkers and those internet apostles.

NOW ARE WE CRAFTING OUR FUTURE OR JUST PATCHING IT UP?

Welding together tomorrow with broken pieces of spirit
wielding pressure and probability
essence, accountability
struggles in solidarity
standing on my humility
don't do it
so fluid
flow til I turn bluish
sinking in it
a young C.S. Lewis, I'm thinking in the spirit;
there's worlds in the wardrobe!

Coddling verbs
tugging a nerve
waiting, debating the ruins

LIKE... LISTEN UP!

There's castles in those clouds
building an airship and paint it like Warhol
now I'm sailing pop culture and all your peers get stoned like adulterers;
a digital generation
works opposing the vultures
that poke holes in my culture
I paint my lows with emulsion
a new canvas to write my stance in a stanza
they tried to eat me with slander but I told you the dark can't hurt me
you know all of my secrets, they flow through the speakers
I broke all of my demons, plenty gnashing of teeth and
my thesis like anaesthesia

I wrote in the colour of Freedom
what's the world you perceive in
I've found a word to believe in
to drag my nerve and esteem back.

THE LIGHTS

when the money goes
everything deemed dim and
you'd die to see those lights again

my greatest fear is life's surprise
that I won't greet death with staring eyes
how could they dim those starkly lights
without me even seeing

when the money goes
everything deemed dim and
you'd die to see those lights again

Hero has a sister
whose seductive ways are dark within
you'll chase your tail
between your legs
to see colour as bright as then
autonomy now dead to impulse
the partisan
dull
parts far from him

when the money goes
everything deemed dim and
you'd die to see those lights again

never
no light in empty space
from art-lofts
to impoverished places
a glimpse of sin for inspiration's sake
might be the bitter-sweetest taste

in Bewilder's name and all its might
the darkling daze starts harvesting

the money left my next of kin
don't die to see those lights again

Basquiat dabbled in the art
did good with time and lived his shine
overdosed on dreams too quick to cease
and lost his life without a plea

the routine-hit
too tripped my father
but he left in time to flee the darkness
is he really any less of an artist
for surviving night with disfigured mind
now he reimagines shape
myself too
trying to find my way
loneliness
addiction
shame
are three tired tyrants the same

an inward gaze paints solipsism
connecting to others' portraits your pain
a second shot to shy the shade
when all you've lost
is all you've gained

art-friends leave
like drug-friends do
all said and done
the game is played
but when the money goes
everything's deemed dim
I'll adjust my eyes
to see light
again

FROM OUR ARMS

The sensation of deep sleep is how I imagine you left us
a feeling like awakening from a dream and the narrative ending
the phenomenon of fluttering eyelids and rays of light flooding in like rainfall
empty holes that suddenly expand their levees
piling up drops of information, dictating a new day
no more.

You left us
but never without waving goodbye
and in every stroke of skin that cut
through cold air like tides of water
you filled the room with your love.

Reality didn't escape you at all
you prepared us by knitting away at a legacy
of compassion, empathy,
joy and warmth
every day around the sun you skated with a purpose of sparing people time
you graced us a love that you were never taught to bear.

I hope you managed to get some rest last night
for fighting such a war of tenacity and passion for life
is enough to make the body tired
you surpassed surviving and nurtured a means of thriving
beyond means
carving out smiles
spelling out hope
and imprinting it on everyone your existence could encompass.

I'm so thankful that I was able to experience you
from plates of pancakes
to treasured walks in the park
and the way you always left space to listen.
If there was ever a story unabridged
it's yours

and I thank you for giving us the chance
and drive
to write our own.

UNPARALLELED FRIEND, A FIRE

It's been 24 hours since I've eaten
and 72 hours since I've felt the presence of
the most important entity of love in my life
the hunger pains for the latter are far worse.

I've tossed & turned every sleep or lack thereof
I can't shift boulders of thought
I'm frightened by life and time apart from you.

You've been my staple diet
you've fed me, nourished me
draped me down in garments of comfort
you've stripped me down to my core
even when it was claustrophobic
I suffocated and returned for more
you've questioned all my ideals
the ordeals of tested preconception
you've pulled at all my strings
I've grown and passionately
exhaustingly I love
with you boredom is barren.
This version of myself hasn't felt the cold side of solitude
without your solace.

The city is no fun without you
and I find my way to salvage a piece of you
lighting up in every abyss-ridden crack and crevasse.

Every song I've heard a hundred times
every varied shade of grey in slabs of concrete, I meander
every ache in my skeleton
every pun echoing my skull
every person I loathe and like
every rhyme for your name

every species I translate into your tongue
everything feels like a story worth telling to you.

A friend who is a fire
that has burnt on for lifetimes before me
you've shifted shapes and stared down skies
that alternate & recalibrate
washing away old for new by the season.

Fire can't be tamed
nor can I ask you to stay here
but the fire that is you, I've chosen.
I hoped you'd blaze with me for every grasp of air
I can bear to breathe beside your heat.

If I blew out my last breath
before cradling your ardent warmth again
I'd regret my pride that stood between us
and my fear of change that sent you away.

I can't be the voice of your past
and your searing wounds I try to sew shut
keep on bursting open.
I can't cool you off
and I won't put you out
a fire of my own I must nurture
but I hoped we could burn
burn together
forever and further.

DAYDREAM

My mind is fireproof
I don't follow no rules nor conventions
I just tackle this life sentence with a sentence
as a matter of fact
take off the tyres too
we must have a bumpy ride to our future
riding through the hardship that never tarnished our shiny boots
jumping through nooses and rings of fire where
you can meet the higher you
9 to 5s divide us but you've got fight left inside of you
never let them silence you

Our dreams are worth much more than the attention we pay them
much more than pensions
tensions
and hair extensions and henchmen
use whatever existential utensil you must
to strengthen your thoughts
this life is but a breathing illusion and
the only solution is to bury the corpse
of course
to hide from the fact that we are alive when we die
besides bodily decomposition there's a whole new composition that starts

The art of returning home
the Prodigal Son with a gun
heading back to the place from which he came
on his way he must stand with no shame for his Father's name
to start a new life of
love
or pain

The life & times of
the oddities of
the perplexities of
the lunacies of
the paradoxes of
people-made personas &
their perspectives

THE ETERNAL COMMUTE

I'm trapped inside a moving cage
being force-fed the manuscript of corporate gossip
pronounced gospel
shovelled with a southern drawl.
There's no liberation from these voices
their dialects fluctuate and inflect
like evangelical preachers professing prophetic scripture
but this sermon seems sort of empty

Networking
Ambiguity
She's so middle class
It's not a popularity contest
Have you eaten your croissant?

She kicks the back of my spaceship of solitude
when oxygen and gravity are no more
in every instant she excites herself with her colleague's downspiral

When you're an artist from the north
and the vibrancy of capital spaces calls you
the commute is eternal
the urinal shutters over potholes in tracks and rails
so sometimes I splash my shoes

Awaiting judgement
I sweat and shiver through climate change
the air conditioning hurtles my body into survival mode
the ceiling begins to liquidise and drip down the walls and on to my face
I THINK THE GOSPEL IS INFILTRATING MY BRAIN
my mental health is a plate of melting blancmange
functioning off one
and only one
hour's sleep

Some pretend hell is pleasant
in first class they crack open bottles of Pinot Grigio at any sign of daylight
they sink capitalist gnashes into crumbling chocolate tiffins
and connect to outside world civilisations with electrical current

pondering
currency and stock exchange

A Japanese man so suave
flicks through SMS messages from parents
on sensitive-to-touch state-of-the-art tech
straight out of Silicon Valley
he's crafting his pitch proposing 5-star luxury accommodation
for postgraduate studies
proclaiming fees fed by globalisation
and dominating target markets will actualise this
but the text is vertical and eligible to the foreign eye
so stereotypes do whisper assumed truths

THE GOSPEL RINGS OUT

It's halitosis
It's truly, truly horrific
When you stop breathing but the smells still seep through

As I begin to tune out
my cage comes to a jittering halt
and I'm welcomed into a whole new noise
from prisoner
to miner

Underground stations like the sunken cities of Atlantis but
these citizens gulped up all residue of life

In small cities people don't keep to their left or right
we just migrate spaces in our own time
here people pile on top of people

without room to swim
and no water to drown

Overpopulated polite queues
and direction queries
echo and repeat themselves through time here

There's always an American and Yorkshireman lost in London

the poet's work riddled with malaprops

stoic work nursing the paradox

No name
blank script
No name
the man in the mirror doesn't correlate with me on the other side of the glass
No name
does the Earth hear my shout?
No name
does this meaning bear meaning itself?
Is existence clear on the other side of it (eschatology)?
No name
no brain you give yourself to shamefulness
No name
does the pendulum remain stagnant when you don't fearfully watch it
catching its every breath
resting its very being for when we obsess over it next?

No name
do you call me by slave or king?
is my album titled 'unknown' in your playlist of greatest hits?
No name
when you tag me on socially unsocial media do the letters match my character
do the 140 characters do justice to my character?
No name

What's the rush late for work work for nothing nothing to live for
live for nothing
die and lose it all
play with fire get fired risk it all 1 out of 15 thousand employees
unemployed
no one knows me
No name
leave home where the heart is left heartless where's your passion
left it at home
alarm clock went off late responded to my alarm clock too late
just didn't register overslept skipped register
No name
go to bed earlier

can't sleep wake up tired
if you wake up dead
don't wake up at all
don't overdo it don't underdo it
fumble for balance
moderation is good it's good to be modest
believe in yourself
stand up for what you believe in
'my name is' DON'T BE SO SELFISH
No name
say what you think
I think you're a [CENSORED]
narcissist
WAKE UP what are you narcoleptic done too much narcotics
'no I don't smoke or drink' what a square
loosen up thought we were tight
jeans too baggy jeans too tight
pull them up pull them down DON'T BE SO GROSS, SEXIST [CENSORED]
'I don't talk to women like that I respect them' HA HA lollolol [CENSORED]
No name

I just need someone who can obey and comply
come on think outside the box don't be such a yes man
'Do you like this design' NO 'well you're wrong'
No name

Anything's possible be realistic
what will you eat you'll eat your words
half full hurry up half empty things aren't that bad
he said 'you'll do it if you love me' she said 'if I do it will you love me?'
no answer
No name

Everything happens for a reason
'what's the matter why aren't you talking to me' no reason
No name
don't be such a sheep follow me on Twitter

everyone's different what a hipster Mr

No name

Speak your mind I won't shoot you for it

can you think your thoughts silently please

Born in a place where they treat uniqueness contrary to what is deemed
the norm (as so they should)

The thoughts of The Other cascade the globe's layer in search of a shade
of land they can call their home

His name is X the shoe doesn't fit

His name is X wrong class

His name is X

not limited to generation X but Y and Z

as a matter of fact X exists in every culture class and country

in every walk of life

the day doesn't quite cast the same impression on him as it
does his peers

the ways things appear only have him peer into a new reality

that doesn't align with what you see smell or hear

new acquisitions new trends new fads 'Indigo?'

NO

no new age new page new slave airy fairy rationale is required

no reformed redefined definition need be acquired

the price is paid so

you might stumble over adjectives and

mumble muddled words to

try and make us fit into your world but

the truth is we made words

We sculpted the A

We tummy tucked the B

We bent back the C

we are the innovators

we are brass players

we are play-writers

play-fighters stage-divers

we're not the industry we donated to the industry

we're the ministry

we're the sit-in-the-back-row people
we're the we-thought-we-were-average-joe people but we're
not we're the backstage stars
the songs you hear on the radio are probably ours
I made your idol shine
I wrote the #1 single from your favourite artist
I co-directed your favourite movie
I'm the new and improved you
I'm the yesterday of your tomorrow
I'm the Ludwig whose symphonies were never published
I'm the Picasso who never caught a break even after the grave
I'm the scrolls of Socrates that were burnt and cindered
I'm the kid that lingered in dark corners of the classroom
the best you've never heard
I'm the revolution that didn't quite spark change
I'm the innovation that didn't quite make it off the ground
AND I'M PROUD
They crucified me I'm not the same
They wouldn't let me through their Pearly Gates I'm not the same

No name who cares
No name no one there
No name to blame

I don't want to be an extension of His story
I won't go down in history
this is My story

the unknown novelist
the incognito invention
the masqueraded author
the back-story of fameless matterless matter
the beauty in the abyss
the something in nothing
the uninspired inspiration
the lifeless resurrection
the asthmatic respiration

the needless desperation
the contradictory fact
the truth trapped in a paradox
giving strength to the feeble imagination
a nameless generation
we need no name
our name ought not be told
therefore our name could never be scorned

'Jenny?' HERE
'John?' HERE
'James?' Here
'X?'

Yours sincerely,
No name

EXISTENTIALISM

This is an accumulation of thoughts and feelings suppressed
I held a cannon to the head of the apathetic side of self I detest
I told him I had to get this off my chest
I've been pacing steps in a circular motion
he begged and pleaded and called on demons
from different regions of this internal bleeding
I told him emotions are like seasons
and yours is Autumn
your reign has fallen now

This horsepower is motion
and it tortures morsels of fear inside my dreams

I met the world's most considerate drug dealer
he asked me what I need...
he cared
I said unfortunately nothing that your product could provide for me
he told me how all he needed was some change
I told him that I needed the same
but I don't think I'll find myself Abel in that Cain
more of an enemy than a brother
you'll never find happiness in those white lines
like you won't find truth in those white lies
and I can't walk around with an open mind all the time
certain things evoke closing hours
it's only normal Mr Pushaman GURU
it's only normal

I shouted
'Nothing's for free right?'
as I passed him by and disappeared into the night so aloof
mostly I feel like life's a ruse and time's a truce
I bite the bullet and tie the noose
STOP!
all thoughts are reversible but actions are not

and my thoughts on you must be so obtuse because I can't seem
to get the right angle
my pride dangles at the gallows whilst my mind's tangled
and all I can do is watch like
'Do something! Why you just standing there?
Why are you all just standing there watching me?'
What is this some sort of sick puppet show?
Where I prostitute my highs and lows in a cage closed
in the name of a stage show
and still can't earn a penny
NO!
This is freedom!
So, how come when I say rap all you hear is

TRAP TRAP

If you're seeing what I'm seeing
this is Eden
I'm talking temptations and teachings
and preachings
appeasing this piece of peace inside of me
Ephesians
letters
numbers
syllables that stumble over themselves
to try and deliver their true meaning
because trying's better than quitting right?
I mean that's what they told me
they told me trying's better than quitting
but what happens when effort and ethos don't
quite stretch and sheer genuinity can't run the
mile on your behalf alone so
before you lose interest in me
here's something that I need you to know
and it's that you don't know me
and it's impossible to lose interest in something that you never knew

that's just how some people choose to live their life
never revealing true strands of self in fear of temporality
I'm not immune to this
we all build up wa ls
I'm guilty
with that being sa d
yes, someday this place will suffocate my flame
but until then
I'll burn bright
so keep your eyes on me

This is an accumu ation of thoughts and feelings expressed
I freed the apathetic side of self I once repressed.

SHIFTING SANDS

Touch ground like a new man
old friend full of old demons
not sure I can exercise them
head down at a cold zenith

not sure that I know myself
but assured you don't know me either
yet you're surprised that advice
that you comprised
depleted

I can't surmise that all the words
that leave your lips aren't lies and
I can see myself inside the things I've criticised

Living life on a lonely edge
no friends trying to talk me down
my delusions of grandeur expand until they break my body
bound

Purpose is a hobby cloud
gripe shy as I grown and frown
I'd love to roll around but I'm on the ledge
burnt to the marrow
a mess

my choice is as narrow as death
I'd love to wallow way less
over sorrow
dead morals and stress
I barely ponder at most
I'd like to visit the coast
write novels on hollow postmodern distress

Man shakes in the cold street
asks me for some spare change
I said *pray tell, I've seen myself through better days*
I proclaimed that I have nothing
implying that I've got something
because nothing is freedom to think and that's a victor's trumpet

There's a child in every adult commuting
the imposter in the mirror is gruelling
every dream takes me closer to wiser but
every dream is just a dream that is fleeting

the wall cries tears in the dark
painted by shadows of the rain that
drip down panes of glass reflecting the city's pain

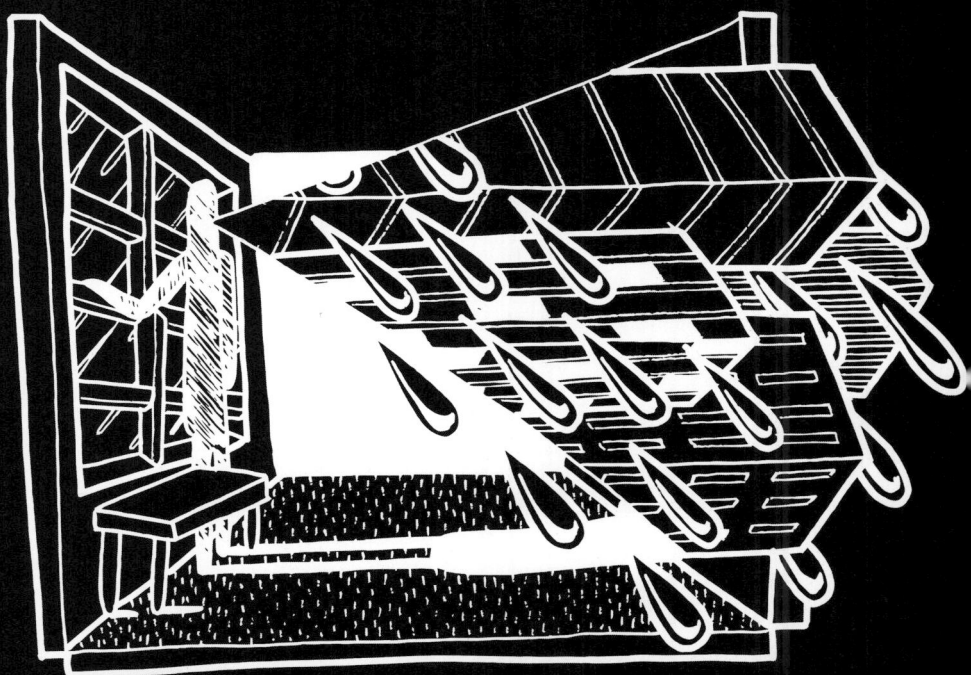

OH JANE

followed by a feeling
stalked
stark
jump to the sky and swallowed by the ceiling
but my potential never did align with reality

I know everyone talks about the power of the centred
present moment but
some of my most treasured segments of time were spent in episodes of
nostalgic bliss and reminiscence
so I could never deny them their imperative

I thought I was mourning moments in time
and then it struck me
I was mourning the people that defined those moments
some moments experienced feel as though they
hold existence as individual lifetimes within the life in which we live now
these lives are where we love

Sometimes I feel like happiness is a fleeting visitor
only in town for the night
she's gone before I wake
most mornings I overslept
most days
I miss her

NO ONE HERE HEARS ME

How loved you must be to bathe in the security of a social circle
I rot here
No one ever really hears me.

Indulge me compliments on my social skill
everybody tells me the secrets that distort their reality
when left unspoken but
No one ever really hears me.

I fear the pen
I'm more than conscious of its power
it could be said I'm obsessed with the craft and mastery
pulling worlds from words encapsulated in pin-drops on pathways
but the story I never feel I do justice
everyone expects something profound of me and still
No one ever really hears me.

When I spit venom in my mind
about how you thrive under the privilege of friendship
my cadence spills with cushioned pretence
I fall through black holes inside myself and drown in introspection
I watch reflections of my falling self plummet deeper
this bitter smile's driving me
No one ever really hears me.

I gave you signs
I wrote you songs
I scribbled symbols of a lack of love on creators of false hope
I chased dreams that didn't save me
I left the brush by the easel
I've woven tapestry seething with imagery
teasing post-existence but
No one ever really hears me.

I don't know where to go from here
I've fallen for ideas
and built my life around ideals that alluded truth
but I feel so unearthed
I feel otherworldly
I feel
No one ever really hears me.

I sewed my mouth shut and sang hymns of brokenness
I bled through the cracks in my lips where the stitching ripped
I wept tears from everywhere except my eyelids
my fingertips can't feel home
I clutch your hand but I'm never really here
I'm lost in universes of parallel worlds
where people recite my speeches and instigate movements of revolt
inspired by the drip from my tongue.

I feel nothing and something in the same instance
being that I felt myself where no one could reach
I loosen the knot below my cranium cap
I swing my last dance of daydream and preach the same sermon over
to pews filled with nothing but empty bags of dust.
I've mulled over time and time again
the moment I thought of a fish trapped inside my skull
swimming around in its bowl
and how the music swept my body with waves of sound
distilled with rhythm
oh how my head bangs to staccato triplets
I remember how the bowl broke
I'm reminded daily by the shattered fragments of denatured shards
floating round my dome
they slice every glimmer and glimpse of thought worth extrapolating
from this volt of loneliness
in exclusion where contentment is seldom
No one ever really hears me.

I hope this coach that carries my shell doesn't crash
though I imagine it did
I know I'm writing like you
and how you hate that you write like this
but I love it when you do.

THE BARBER

In memory of Trevor Darien, aka Mr T
1963–2018

If ten men interview for a vacancy
where five men are clean-shaven and the other half let nature be
reality has it that the five men shaven are ready for the world
a clean face must paint a thousand canvases
statistics show that these men have a higher likelihood of employment
as if shadows of carpeted skin hide away truth
this means that physical aesthetic
and those hunger pangs in the stomach of your children
are one and the same

A well-shaven man meets expectation
I learnt this in a barbershop
I like to spend time here
these men walk with a certain integrity
I could only reserve for trying to convince my legs to move
they sow seeds of new beginnings so sovereign
and talk the folklore like a sort of absolute
there's an untold beauty in the poetry of these people

The community philosopher
shaves seconds from days
perfecting his hypothesis
one of solemn
one of practice
there's a beauty

Shed the old;
a man with a clean-shaven beard has a healthy mind
and a barber is a therapist

Both neighbours on both sides own Chinese eateries
and when they leave town they give their children the number of The Barber

the kids call him uncle
a Black man relative to East Asian offspring
trust and community
two concepts usually too scarce to mention
but sincerity is woven in the actions of the man that shaves heads
of the hurt
reformed
wealthy and poor
he emphasises with ease
a lot of hours spent talking to people
he upholds morality and responsibility in the way he debates news headlines
and holds you accountable for public welfare

Outside the shop stand two sociology graduates
arguing equality
'so post-oppression and evolved'
so much so that you have more than double the chance
of employment
if the bodies of your predecessors were pushed out
on the side of the sun that scorched your skin less

A well-shaven man makes for friendly custom
and fairer skin makes for virtuous living
Black clouds command rain that waters life
while black magic is practiced most by white imperialists

My grandmother reads *The Guardian*:
'Race remains the most commonly recorded motivation for hate crime
at 82 per cent of recorded motivations'
and don't we all crack the whip in unspoken thought

A well-shaven Black man might consider self-employment
over a free-to-roam white male

Sometimes the most valuable knowledge, wisdom and
meaning can be found in the most humble of places.

WORRIES

I condemn the part of me that advocated 24 hours of procrastination
such thought lacks in pros
and sows in crass

Every bone in my mind aches
every muscle in my soul whimpers
and still I stand with no solution

Ever wonder how worries travel
they pulsate through insecurities that breach their restraint
my perception pleads that they have long overstayed their welcome
they shout over gavel stomps
attempting to make their case for sheltered courage and
buried confidence
they hide their reasoning in perplexity
unfamiliar emotion
and wilder
they pierce wounds in self-knowledge
and 'tis here where worries build their kingdom
and drive their reign

Express how you feel
but first understand how you feel
I preach to myself sat in pews
Burn canyons in self-doubt
Waste essence Not
Barter with time Not
Do so Now

Cut down stems of despondence
Rebuild structures of replenish
Reform the right to believe
and watch worries hurtle from high places
and slowly
wither away

THE LIFE OF A SECOND

What if every second was a conscious, autonomous, rational thinking being
whose home was the Present
whose purpose was simply to Be and that is all
whilst other elements of existence possessed the complexity of to Do
Seconds would know to Be is simple
they'd know you can't Be any other way
or Be with greater or less potential
to Be is pure, whole, complete
in essence and actuality.

What if every Second had a family or colony that extended up to 60 members
and these motley crews were named Minutes
what if Seconds dwelled in small villages that occupied up to 3,600 Seconds
called Hours
what if Seconds attended Time School where they'd learn not to be wasted
they'd learn how to escape losing themselves
avoiding the vortex of squander
what if in this world the only constant or natural law is that Time passes
the great inevitable.

What if every Second knew within itself that Time was relative as intuition
what if student Seconds of Time School would dream of moving to Days;
a Second's city
where 86,400 Seconds currently live, love, learn, colonise and inhabit
they'd move in hope of being individual
to break free from the pack as an attempt to revolt
against the systems of Time
what if certain Seconds considered themselves populists
and yearned to live a life of balance and equal spread, where time is shared
every Second should have a say in how itself is spent
what if seconds were more than strokes of a pendulum on the face of a clock.

What if Seconds were in fear of how little time they actually had
so much so that they would become immediately startled at the very thought
of a nanosecond

or tremble over a millisecond knowing
their time would soon be up
what if the Past is a Second's death
where its animation ceases to be
what if Memories are life after death for a Second
knitting together their post-existence.

Imagine if photos (although wilted by light with no immunity against Time)
are actually a Second's haven
their heavenly home to return to
what if holes in the Hippocampus where neural pathways fail to make history
are like fire and brimstone for a Second.

What if we spared time mercy like humanity.
If only we spared humanity more time.

THE GREAT EPHEMERAL

Raindrops pile in potholes with pride
as though they pierce the concrete themselves

Seasons dance like we do emulating the great ephemeral

Yesterday's skyscrapers lay mosaic heaps now
tiny mountains modest enough to carpet our path

Don't we all wield hands with butterfly-effect fingertips

Barren are the hilltops and heavens without the humility to love

So welcome the stranger you were before the caress of friends
like a strange unfamiliar winter
born summer again.

FLOWERS

do you love flowers
see this here is a question that's plagued my mind for eternity now
do you love flowers
in today's new age
in this land of plastic beauty
robotic pastime and expensive jewellery
what role do flowers play and do you love flowers

could I steal a smile with a Daffodil
could I lend a hand with a Daisy
could I land a kiss with a Rose
do you love flowers

would you prefer a blood diamond or a home-grown Begonia
a botanist is a wordsmith
who crafts his speech of wisdom in the nurturing of a Lily
or plants his legacy with a Tulip
a petal a day
a stem for the soul
the way we grow or
the way we grow apart
leaves me pondering over the question
do you love flowers

if you loved flowers
I'd offer a Marigold for your lows and
a Sunflower for your highs
I'd heal awkwardness with an Orchid
I'd pick Bluebells for those blue days
the scent of Lavender would chase all midnight blues away
Carnations on celebrations and
Heather to weather any storm but
I'm not sure whether or not you love flowers

could I hold happiness in a bunch
could I rest passion by the window
could I place beauty in a vase
a Dahlia to hold memories
a Dandelion to blow away sorrow
we could spell the future in fallen Cherry Blossom
flushes of pink would read the palms of our roots
see, I'm not sure you love flowers
but please, someone tell me it's not true because
if you loved flowers
I'd give one to you

TOGETHERASONE

Dear what feels like an extension of me
you've muted my anxiety
When my eyes set gaze on your light
I find I've lost my fear of feeling less of myself
even though accompanied by the feeling of another

I know you're separate
my eyes verify your essence beyond me
I know you'll exist outside this space in time
but for this moment you've tuned the pieces of my puzzle
you've reminded me of my togetherness
and what it feels like to be in one place
You see my mind has

      wandered   wondering
ever since it grew legs of thought;
chasing its name and idyllic dreams

Your love is rest
restitutive
tearing down walls of insecurity

I've found picturesque home in you
and better yet
with you

This gratitude is appreciation
is non-situational
is ever-changing
is non-quantifiable by time
and this feeling
even if channelled through mediums of reminiscence
will remain

I've found an inability to express vulnerability is disability
so with these words of self-discovery
discovered through someone else
I write to hold this feeling in a capsule that stands as proof
there's always hope
and my poems inspired by love
are as great as my poems inspired by helplessness
Togetherasone.

Facebook isn't your friend
Twitter isn't your follower
and the world doesn't have a friendly leader.

Today I broke my writer's block
and abandoned the rat race
from the starting blocks.

WITHOUT THE COMPUTER

An obsession with time shadows my existence, it stalks my stark reality.
The only light at this point floods in through the format of liquid crystal
display; the inescapable technological comfort, a late 21st-century reliever,
friend to the lonely. Most are no longer able to acknowledge such loneliness.
We've become desensitised by a synthetic community of images, capsules
of data that tell us otherwise. Loneliness only exists in the shaded areas
of our subconscious; we try our best to keep it buried and prevent it from
showing its gruesome face. I, on the other hand, face the beast that is
solitary head on. It's been that way for as long as I can remember.

As the words form
as the ink spills
my pain dissolves.
It's my method.

There exist only two types of people in this world: creators and critics and
then a system that works like a polar shift inclining an individual to one side
more so than the other. My greatest fear is losing my sense of purpose and
slipping into the cracks of comfort which lie in the life of a critic.

To be a creator of anything is to go against the brain's natural state
of comfort. I, for one, believe that today's modern mind is no longer
programmed for survival alone but for maximum comfort and longs to
be in a state of contentment. Now, some would regard contentment
a positive quality; however, to be content 'in a state of happiness and
satisfaction' is to lose motion, therefore requiring no further call for
change and closely associated with change progression.

To create is to progress
to step to the mark of purpose
conflicting with our nature and state of being.
I guess this is the magnetic field and tug of war inside all of us.
Trapped inside a paradox
or is this paradox trapped inside me
eating me from the inside.

SOMEONE IS EVERYONE

Often
I feel like this life is a contradiction
a constant constriction from systems that have visions for its prisoners
entrapment
enslaved
and boxed in
watching the clock spin
praying for just a minute where time would stand still but
the hustle
the bustle
the motion
commotion
composes a symphony of chaos
causing decomposition and comatose but
really are we conscious of the content of our consulate or
simply
subconsciously
subtracting common from common sense because
it's becoming less common to possess a sense of common sense
fashion sense is condescending and
if it was Cassius Clay's day
what would Cassius Clay say? probably
'Float Like A Butterfly' but
they touched my wings and they plucked my strings and they
cut my skin

Liberty lives in shackles
Passion has passed its peak
Devotion devours its creed
Confidence can't speak in a room full of broken dreams
Honesty told a lie and
honestly
even eternity's passing by
no need for punctuation right

we're all living in the fast lane
no need to be punctual either
for such a race bears no finish line

Like a scribbled stickman
suited and booted in a black silk tuxedo
draped down in jewels
only to be erased off the page
rubbed into non-existence
WHYSOPESSIMISTIC
they stole optimism and rebranded it as mystic
and sold it to our children
if they believe it
perhaps he's autistic
ADHD
Overactive Mind Syndrome
Fantasy Prone Personality Disorder but
I don't need no PhD to see that I'm not free
if you keep labelling me

YOUSEE

Their #1 rule was to know thy self but
what if that means knowing that I'm nothing without someone else
someone meaning everyone because
there's always someone out of everyone
that plays a role in making up the anatomy of you
there's always someone out of everyone that shaped your view
your perspective
your opinions and
yet you fail to see you're under everyone's dominion
see the heart can't be without the brain and
the brain can't be without the heart so
when things get inflamed
the brain tells the heart not to start and
the heart beats until it beats the brain

this has been going on from the core of time
never before have they learnt to
settle the score

SO

when we go out to war
we're really declaring war against ourselves and
when we murder our brother
we're really stringing the noose up ourselves and
when we spend 23 hours a day out of the 24
on the internet
we're really losing touch with ourselves
as well as everyone else

WE WERE NEVER DERELICT

Pockets of people's stories
cradled by brick and mortar
amidst the rubble and murmur
living catalysts of love

Paint gallons of life on dreary
dance over mundane & void
solitude birthed a smile
that sought community & good

Build towers of noise aside us
such transience won't quake
a spirit, not stone cemented
but blood & flesh & faith

We were never derelict
just displaced and out of sight
carrying home inside us
when home they tried to break

AUTHOR BIOGRAPHY

Otis Mensah, self-proclaimed mum's house philosopher and rap psalmist, offers an alternative take on contemporary Hip-Hop and spoken word. Endeavouring to shed light on existential commonalities through vulnerable expression, Otis's work reads like a stream of consciousness, using aesthetic language to paint worlds of thought.

Otis continues to release music independently, taking creative projects like *Rap Poetics* to the stage around the UK and Europe, as well as making his debut at Glastonbury Music Festival. Throughout his career, Otis has opened for heavyweights like Benjamin Zephaniah, Arrested Development, The Sugarhill Gang, Wu-Tang Clan affiliate Killah Priest, Lowkey, Open Mike Eagle, Chali 2na and Blu & Exile.

ACKNOWLEDGEMENTS

The last few years have been both enriching and humbling and I owe bouquets of gratitude to so many people, both motivators and mentors, on this inspiriting journey.

First off, I'd like to thank our former Lord Mayor and MEP, Magid Magid, not only for gifting me the honour of being Sheffield's first poet laureate, but for respecting my art and the culture of Hip-Hop it stemmed from enough to see its meaning. Magid's work in Sheffield has been profound and disturbing to systems of tradition in need of dismantling. A legacy of community that leaves me feeling inspired and at home.

I'd like to thank my parents, Naomi Mensah and Scott Corrie, for unwavering support of an artistic path sometimes frightening and uncertain, for their encouragement, belief and undoubted artistic influence. To my nan, Gill Flinton, for always helping me alter my perspective for betterment, pushing me further into my study and always supporting me and my curiosity for language. To my grandparents Sharon and John Strutt, for always caring to enquire into my creative practice and supporting me on my way.

A huge howl of thanks to Raluca de Soleil for being an ear to my ideas, tirelessly helping me achieve my goals and filling the road with candour, humour and zeal. To Miroslav Kiss (GRIT MULTIMEDIA) for being a friend, creative partner and offering his creative genius to build visual worlds around my music and words. To Mathis Peckedrath (the intern) for accompanying my kooky poetry with his innovative musicianship, for providing a creative refuge in the shape of his Berlin studio and for a friendship like no other. To Dr Alex Mason for his mentorship, giving me the confidence to deliver my first public lecture and his commitment to breaking down barriers of access in university spaces.

Thank you to the University of Sheffield, BBC Radio Sheffield, BBC Introducing, Off the Shelf, Migration Matters Festival, *Now Then Magazine*, *Exposed Magazine*, Our Favourite Places, VIBE Sheffield, *Pink Wafer*, Our Mel, Blancmange Lounge and many more, for the constant support during my time as poet laureate.

Thank you to Alumno Group for commissioning the poems 'We Were Never Derelict' and 'The Great Ephemeral', and to Being Human

Festival, the work of Dr Maglaque and Amy Carter for commissioning the poem 'Shifting Sands' for Dreaming in Renaissance Italy.

I'd like to thank the beautiful minds in and around Sheffield, the UK and Europe for coming to every show, streaming every song and reading every word. Your support and time truly means the world to me. Thank you for helping piece together my lifelong dream and for the exchange of emotion that keeps me afloat.

Finally, thank you to Jess Chandler, for her endless efforts to champion independent thinking, independent artists and innovative literature with Prototype Publishing and for this opportunity to share my musings.

ABOUT PROTOTYPE

poetry / prose / interdisciplinary projects / anthologies

Creating new possibilities in the publishing of fiction and poetry through a flexible, interdisciplinary approach and the production of unique and beautiful books.

Prototype is an independent publisher working across genres and disciplines, committed to discovering and sharing work that exists outside the mainstream.

Each publication is unique in its form and presentation, and the aesthetic of each object is considered critical to its production.

Prototype strives to increase audiences for experimental writing, as the home for writers and artists whose work requires a creative vision not offered by mainstream literary publishers.

In its current, evolving form, Prototype consists of 4 strands of publications: (type 1 // poetry) / (type 2 // prose) / (type 3 // interdisciplinary projects) / (type 4 // anthologies).

( )   (   )

ISBN 978-1-913513-02-3

9 781913 513023